SURREY
from the Air

SURREY
from the Air

JASON HAWKES

HALSGROVE

First published in Great Britain in 2010

Copyright © in this publication Halsgrove 2010
Images by Jason Hawkes

British Library Cataloguing-in-Publication Data
A CIP record for this title is available from the British Library

ISBN 978 0 85704 000 8

HALSGROVE
Halsgrove House,
Ryelands Industrial Estate,
Bagley Road, Wellington, Somerset TA21 9PZ
Tel: 01823 653777   Fax: 01823 216796
email: sales@halsgrove.com

Part of the Halsgrove group of companies
Information on all Halsgrove titles is available at: www.halsgrove.com

Printed and bound in Italy by Grafiche Flaminia

INTRODUCTION

*W*hile Surrey is not among the largest of English counties it ranks just outside the top ten in terms of its density of population. This is due to its close proximity to London, being highly favoured as a place to live by commuters. Its affluence is reflected in the many desirable properties and communities, especially those in more rural locations, that are to be found here.

Surrey is a county with a fascinating history, being one of the Saxon shires, and taking its name from the region known to the Anglo-Saxons as the 'Southern Kingdom'. Perhaps its most famous location is Runnymede, site of the signing of the Magna Carta in 1215, a document imposing the rule of law over a reigning monarch and from which Parliamentary democracy grew.

As the photographs in this book show, the county boasts some wonderful buildings, among them many fine country houses including Clandon Park and Hatchlands Park. Hampton Court Palace is one of the world's great buildings, and Surrey is of course home to the renowned Royal Horticultural Society Gardens at Wisley.

Away from major towns such as Guildford, Woking and Camberley there is much delightful rural scenery dotted with quintessentially English villages. The fascinating aerial photographs in this book are selected to provide the reader with an overview of a variety of landscapes and settlements, with many historic sites included – in all providing a fascinating aerial portrait of the county.

The principal attraction of aerial photographs is that they are literally a bird's-eye view, allowing us to look down on the landscape from a perspective that we never normally see. Such pictures reveal to us things that are normally hidden from view, and often surprise us when we find that what we had imagined the layout of the land to be is in reality quite different. The best practitioners of this genre of photography also strive to capture an aesthetic in the images they take, and these pictures, sometimes quite abstract in appearance, are often strikingly beautiful in their own right.

Jason Hawkes is one of the country's best-known photographers specialising in aerial photography. From his base near London he travels worldwide to produce images for books, advertising and design. Since 1991 he has provided photographs for major international companies including Nike, HSBC, Ford, Rolex, Toyota and BP. The images in this book and the sister publications in the series were specially commissioned by Halsgrove.

For more information regarding Jason Hawkes' work visit www.jasonhawkes.com. For a complete list of titles in this series and other Halsgrove titles visit www.halsgrove.com.

At the western edge of Camberley stands the Jolly Farmer roundabout on the A30 (London Road) between Camberley and Bagshot. The roundabout used to be home to a pub of that name.

Left: The view northwards over High Street, Epsom.

Above: The High Street, in the pretty village of Limpsfield. The Bull Inn can be seen bottom right.

Left: Tennis courts create a pleasing mosaic on a summer's evening in Limpsfield.

Above: Leret Way and The Crescent, Leatherhead, looking south.

Left: Bisley is Europe's premier shooting ground. The ranges were moved here from Wimbledon in 1895 after the local MP received a bullet through his top hat!

Above: A film crew shooting on the lake at Virginia Water.

High above the snake-like intertwining of the M3 and the M25 motorways at junction 12.

Left: The Slammer ride at Thorpe Park.

Above: Port Atlantis provides visitors to Thorpe Park with a variety of shops and other facilities.

'SAW - The Ride' takes Thorpe Park visitors on a 55mph thrilling journey along a 700 metre-length roller coaster.

Patient queues at Thorpe Park.

Another kind of thrill is available at the John Battleday Waterski Park adjacent to Thorpe Park.

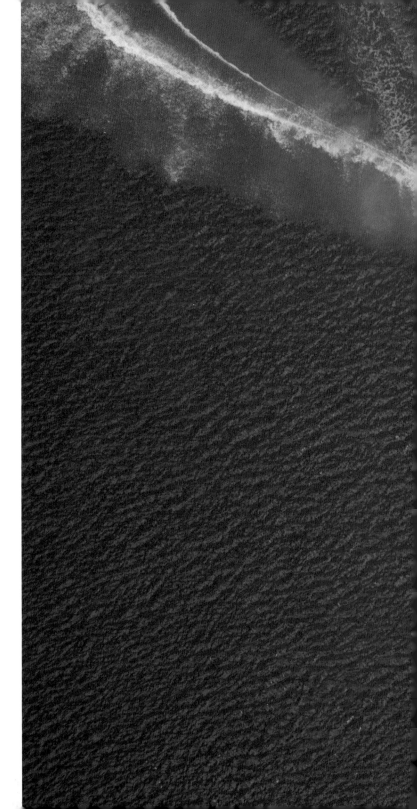

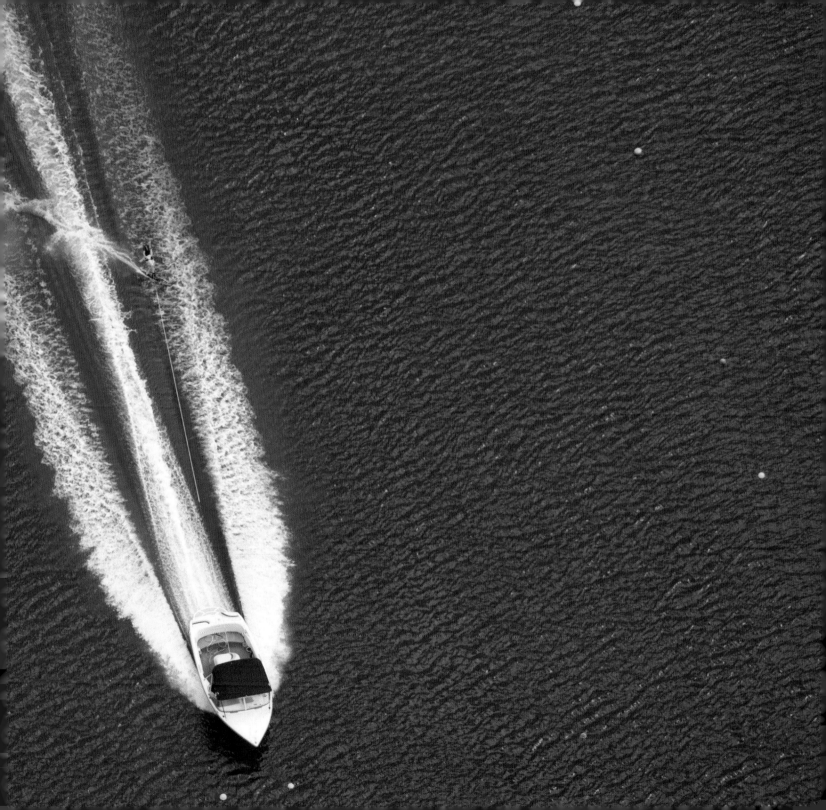

Left and above: The Wentworth Estate near Virginia Water is home to the Wentworth Golf Club. Members have a choice of four courses on which to play, three Championship courses and an Executive course of 9 holes.

Left: The view south over Camberley. This is the fifth largest town in Surrey and is in the Surrey Heath district. The semi-circular Borough Council Offices can be seen bottom left.

Above: St Michael's Church, sits alongside London Road in Camberley.

29

Previous page: A spectacular view looking north-west over the centre of Camberley.

Left: Krooner Park, home to Camberley Town Football Club.

Above: Frimley Park Hospital lies on the southern edge of Camberley alongside the M3 Motorway, just visible bottom left.

Above: Frimley Hatches Nature Reserve. The site comprises four former gravel pits, which have been restored to lakes, most of which are used for angling.

Right: Farnham Castle, lying to the north of the town, dates from 1138. The architecture reflects changing styles through the ages and the castle is one of the most important buildings in southern England.

Left: West Street Farnham can be seen at the centre of this photo-graph which shows the view south over the town.

Above: St Andrews Church, Farnham, sits at the heart of this ancient town.

Above: Another view over West Street, Farnham, near to College Gardens.

Right: Looking back across Farnham to Farnham Castle.

Gostrey Meadow was created in 1910 as a recreational area for the residents of Farnham. There is a children's play area beside the River Wey. The name comes from the 17th century meadows which were known as 'Gostreeds'.

Previous page: The graceful Georgian facade of Waverley Abbey House which lies to the west of Farnham. It is now a training and conference centre.

Left: Waverley Abbey was the first Cistercian abbey in England, founded in 1128. It fell into disrepair following the Dissolution and its ruins are now in the care of English Heritage.

Above: Charterhouse School - 400 years of academic excellence.

Above: The Memorial Chapel at Charterhouse was designed by Sir Gilbert Scott and consecrated in 1927.

Right: The River Wey separates Godalming from Farncombe to the north. This view is of Bridge Road looking from the north into the town of Godalming.

Left: The Burys and the River Wey Godalming. The Rotunda, seen centre, is part of the former Congregational church dating from the mid 1800s and now a listed building.

Above: The view south towards the High Street and the centre of Godalming.

Above: St Peter and St Paul Church, Godalming. A church has stood on this site since the ninth century and carvings survive from that time.

Right: Mesmeric from the air these polytunnels dominate the farming landscape near Busbridge, south of Godalming.

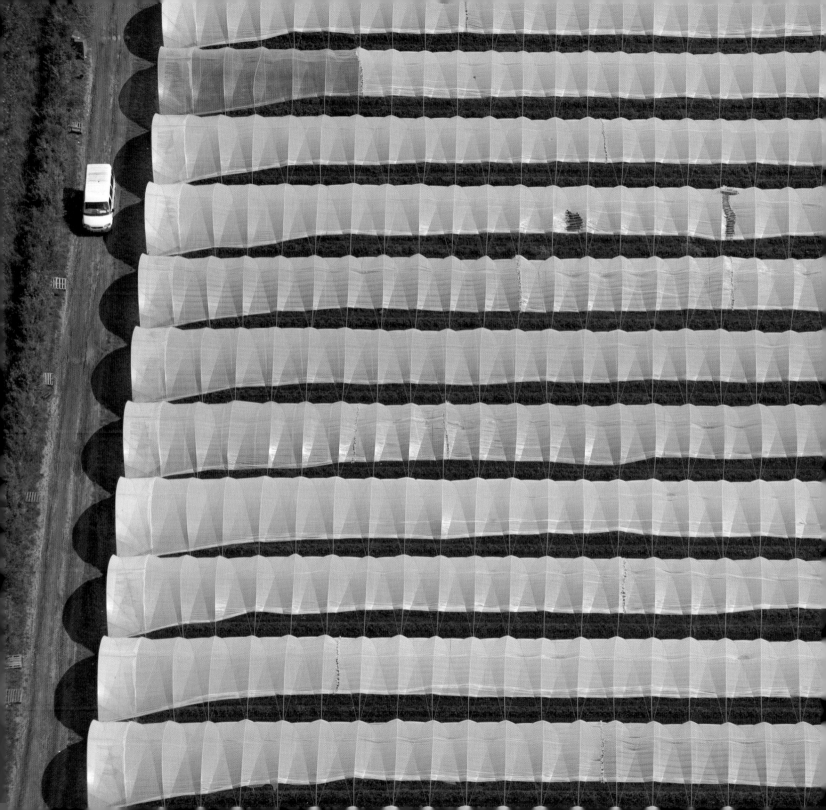

Fruitpickers work amongst row on row of plants at this Busbridge farm near Godalming.

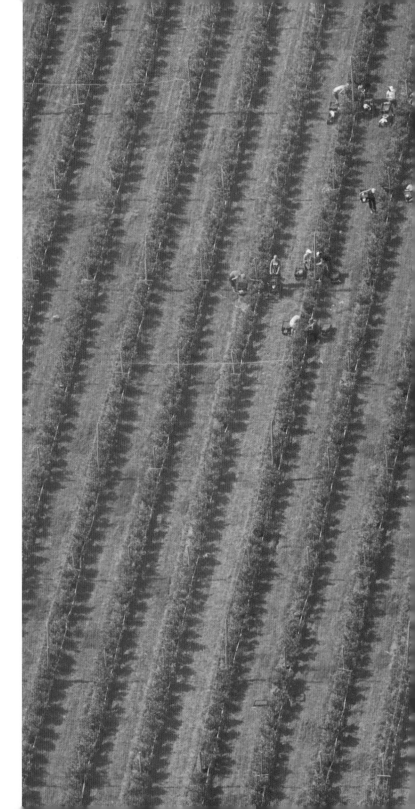

Previous page: Lying west of Godalming the village of Munstead was once served by this water tower, built in 1898. Now a Grade II listed building the tower is converted into a private residence comprising six storeys.

Left and above: The house and gardens at Loseley Park offer visitors a superb day out. The gardens are based on a design by the famed Gertrude Jekyll.

Left: Guildford is the county town of Surrey and is also the largest with a population of around 67 000. This view looks north over Guildford Cathedral and the University of Surrey.

Above: Looking along North Street, Guildford.

Above: St Mary's church Guildford overlooks Quarry Street at the old heart of the original town.

Right: Guildford Castle was built shortly after the Norman invasion of 1066. The gardens surrounding the castle are now a public park and the gatehouse contains a museum.

Above: The River Wey winds alongside Millbrook, Guildford, past the Yvonne Arnaud Theatre seen bottom right.

Right: Abbot's Hospital, Guildford, stands at the edge of the High Street. This magnificent Jacobean building is now used for a variety of community purposes.

Left: Stoke Park, Guildford, is a large public recreational area close to the town centre.

Above: Clandon Park lies to the west of Guildford. Built in the 1730s the house and gardens are now in the care of the National Trust.

Previous page: Hatchlands Park was built for Admiral Boscawen in the 1750s. The house contains superb Robert Adam interiors and houses the Cobbe Collection of keyboard instruments. It is in the care of the National Trust.

Left: Horsley Towers stand in Horsley Park south of East Horsley. Privately owned it is a very popular venue for weddings and other functions.

Above: Effingham lies a few miles east of Leatherhead. The village contains a number of important buildings including the twelfth century church of St Lawrence, seen here.

Above and right: Standing at the edge of the North Downs south of Bookham the house and gardens at Polesden Lacy are in the care of the National Trust. The house dates from the 1820s and the gardens, set in 1400 acres, offer superb views across the Surrey Hills.

70

Above and right: Box Hill takes its name from the box trees which are found on its steep southern and western flanks, most notably around the 'Whites' - chalk cliffs cut by the River Mole. The ruined tower, seen right, is stands among the many paths that criss-cross the area.

Left: Milton Court is a sixteenth century house near Dorking which was substantially redesigned by the Victorian architect William Burges. It is now the offices of a major insurance company.

Above: The view north above Dorking with the spire of St Martin's seen top right.

Norbury Park lies to the south of Dorking. The area provided the inspiration for Fanny Burney's novel *Camilla* and the house was later home of Leopold Salomons JP who gave Box Hill to the nation in 1914. Marie Stopes, famous for her book *Married Love* and for her pioneering work on birth control, resided at Norbury Park for twenty years up to her death in 1958.

Above: The little village of Mickleham appears in the Domesday Book and its church, dedicated to St Michael, is thought to be one of the oldest in the county.

Right: The windmill on Reigate Heath, a mile of so west of Reigate, is possibly the only windmill to have been consecrated as a place of worship. In 1880 it became St Cross Chapel.

Green algae colours the emerald waters of a gravel pit near the village of Buckland that lies midway between Box Hill and Reigate.

Above and right: The children's play area and Pavilion Cafe at Priory Park in Reigate.

Redhill town centre and the Belfry shopping centre. With a population of around 25 000 Redhill is one of the principal towns in Surrey being within the London commuter belt

Left: Looking into High Street, Redhill.

Above: Linear patterns above Redhill station. It lies at the junction of three lines: the main London to Brighton line, the North Downs line, and the Redhill to Tonbridge line.

Previous page: At the junction of the M25 and M23.

Left: Kingswood village is near Tadworth. Now the offices of Legal & General, St Monica's was a former girl's school and, aptly, starred in the St Trinians comedy films of the 1950s and 60s.

Above: Circular street layout at Downland Way, Epsom.

Above: Looking south-westwards over Epsom Downs racecourse and the Duchess's Stand, opened in 2009. This is one of the world's premier racecourses, home to the Derby.

Right: RAC Country Club, Woodcote Park, Epsom. The mansion was built in 1679 by Richard Evelyn, brother of the diarist John.

Above: ExxonMobil is the world's largest publicly owned energy company. The UK headquarters are in Leatherhead at ExxonMobil House.

Right: Looking along the High Street, Leatherhead, at the junction with The Crescent and Elm Road.

Left: Waterway Road bridge and the railway line to Box Hill cross the River Mole in Leatherhead.

Above: The view directly along the High Street and the pedestrianised area of Leatherhead's shopping centre.

Above: St John's public school was founded in 1851 as a school for the sons of the clergy. It was moved from London to Leatherhead in 1871.

Right: The turf maze at RHS Wisley Gardens which lie midway between Leatherhead and Woking.

The garden of the Royal Horticultural Society at Wisley is a 'mecca' for garden-lovers everywhere. This beautiful garden, with romantic half-timbered Tudor-style buildings, includes a canal designed by Sir Geoffrey Jellicoe, a rock garden, formal and walled gardens, mixed borders, a rose garden, rock garden, glasshouses, a fruit field and an arboretum. There are also alpine gardens, the model vegetable gardens and a country garden by Penelope Hobhouse.

Not only pleasing for the gardener and horticulturalist, the formal layout of this part of the garden at Wisley has a particular aesthetic appeal when seen from the air.

Above: The Rock Garden leading to the Alpine Meadow is one of
Wisley's most delightful features.

Right: The Glasshouse.

Previous page: Not far from the village of Pyrford lie the ruins of Newark Priory close by the Abbey Stream. Founded in the twelfth century the abbey fell at the Dissolution. Now a Grade I listed building, the site is not accessible to the public.

Left: Newark Lock on the River Wey Navigation. Originally used for transporting barge loads of heavy goods via the Thames to London, the waterway now forms part of the inland waterway network.

Above: Kingfield Stadium – the home of Woking FC.

Previous page: Narrow boats tied up at Pyrford Marina which lies alongside the Rive Wey Navigation just to the east of Pyrford.

Looking into Woking town centre from above the railway station and The Broadway. The spire of Christ Church can be seen in the centre of the photograph.

The futuristic McLaren Technology Centre in Woking. Designed by the Norman Foster Partnership the building has been described as being 'as high tech and innovative as the Formula 1 cars built inside it'. It even looks like a race track, complete with chicanes and hairpin bends.

Left: Part of the present-day circuit sited at the famous Brooklands race track and airfield.

Above: Wet skid circle at the Mercedes-Benz World, Weybridge. Here visitors can test themselves on a number of circuits driving high-powered cars.

Above: The impressive Mercedes-Benz World building at Brooklands.

Right: Beverley Park golf range near New Malden.

A truly classic view of the Thames and Richmond taken from above
Richmond Hill looking north-west.

Looking south along the River Thames with Kingston-upon-Thames on the left.

Left: A stretch of the River Thames between Teddington Lock and Kingston Bridge. On the right is the Tamesis sailing club.

Above: Hampton Court Palace from the north. The building comprises the Tudor palace developed by Cardinal Wolsey and then by Henry VIII, and the later baroque palace built by William III.

Left: From Bushy Park looking south into East Molesey.

Above: Hampton Court Palace is in the care of Historic Royal Palaces, an independent charity. It is considered to be one of the finest visitor attractions in the country.

Previous page: Ash Island lies in the River Thames adjacent to Molesey Lock at East Molesey. It is privately owned and has a boatyard and moorings.

Left: Opened in 1962 Queen Elizabeth II reservoir is a vital part of London's water supply.

Above: D'Oyly Carte Island once belonged to that famous impresario, producer of the Gilbert & Sullivan operas. It lies between Sunbury Lock and Shepperton Lock, north of Weybridge.

Above: Shepperton Lock and Lock Island.

Right: Hamhaugh Island lies in the River Thames and is mainly residential with a total of 46 houses. Although close to Weybridge, the town can only be reached from the island by boat.

Just north of Weybridge this wier on River Thames lies between Hamhaugh Island and Hamm Court.

Pharaoh's Island was given to Admiral Nelson following the Battle of the Nile. He used it as a fishing retreat. Today the island is rather more densely populated but it remains something of a private retreat being accessible only by boat.

A bird's-eye view of Guildford Street and London Street, Chertsey, with the church of St Peter's centre.